INTRODUCTION TO OPERATING SYSTEMS

Introduction to Operating Systems

Philip Avery Johnson

Hampton University

iUniverse, Inc.

New York Lincoln Shanghai

Introduction to Operating Systems

iUniverse, Inc.

For information address:
iUniverse, Inc.
2021 Pine Lake Road, Suite 100
Lincoln, NE 68512
www.iuniverse.com

ISBN: 0-595-31430-9 (pbk)
ISBN: 0-595-66312-5 (cloth)

Printed in the United States of America

To Margaret, Lori and Jeffrey

Contents

▼

Acknowledgments

I owe a debt of gratitude to a number of people with respect to this book.

First, to John Curtiss and Bob Graham for writing references for me when I was applying to Hampton. John was a former international executive with Dow Chemical and Bob was a former executive with IBM (as well as being a graduate of Hampton University). My thanks to John and Bob for the opportunity to teach and write.

Next to Ralph Clark, another executive (now retired) at TRW. At a Christmas party in 2003, Ralph said something to me that really motivated me to think about writing again. I can't say I recall exactly what he said (maybe it was the Chardonney), but he got me going. Thanks, Ralph!

Next to Patrick Willson, who talked about *God's Gray Glory*. This gave me the motivation, when the going got tough and I needed some help to continue.

Also to Bob Willis, my mentor in the computer science department at Hampton. I had originally interviewed with Bob a number of years ago; he remembered me when I was looking to continue teaching, after William & Mary's funding problems. It has been a joy working with Bob: I am in awe of the motivation that he gives to the young people at Hampton. Thanks to you, Bob.

Lastly, thanks to my wife, Margaret, for putting up with my moods when I'm stuck on what to say and for the loss (or lack) of focus on things that she would like to do. This, too, shall pass.

To paraphrase Shakesphere, motivation to start and to complete comes from many unanticipated places. Thanks, all.

Williamsburg, VA
Spring 2004

CHAPTER 1

▼

INTRODUCTION

This book strives to introduce operating systems to the beginning student in the area of operating systems. Generally, this would be an undergraduate computer science major taking his or her first course in operating systems, but may extend to others that have interest in how computers work. The book will deal with generic issues on the inner workings of operating systems, rather than deal with the specifics of a particular vendor. More specifically, the scope of this book will deal with single-processor systems; multiple-processor systems and most issues involving the Internet and Web are left to others. The one exception is the last chapter, which deals with the client-server operation and its importance to the Internet and Web.

This book will deal with the history of operating systems, the interrupt structure, protection, states of systems, synchronization, memory interactions, file issues and I/O workings. These subjects will be covered roughly in the above order throughout the book. In general, the operating system and its study investigates the inner workings: specifically, how functionality of the hardware is controlled and commanded to do various functions, how the file system (indeed, no system is still a system in this sense) works and how the I/O devices are commanded and controlled to provide functionality from the user point-of-view. It is probably apparent that, as the technology of the hardware has increased in functionality over the years, the attributes of the operating system have changed to keep in step with advances in the hardware. From this point of view, advances in the hardware (or new inventions, such as I/O or virtual memory) have caused changes in the operating system design by necessity. We will have a bit more to say about this in the next chapter on the history. Welcome to the story.

CHAPTER 2

▼

HISTORY

To reiterate, one can define an operating system in the following way: 1) acts as an intermediary between the human user and the computer hardware, 2) manages and allocates resources, 3) controls the execution of programs (sometimes called application programs of the user), 4) controls the operation of I/O devices, and 5) deals with the inter communications between the different parts of the hardware (which the human user generally never sees). As you might expect, different pieces of the above list have evolved over time from the early computers, which had no need for such command and control. But we're getting ahead of our story.

Mainframe Systems

Mainframe systems evolved more or less directly from the single-purpose computer systems (such as the computers used by the U.S. military in calculating artillery paths during World War II and the ENIAC at the University of Pennsylvania). Generally, the human user entered program and data through the computer console, output was typically an LED readout (printers had yet to be developed) . As time went by, people by the mid-1950s were looking for a way to get better production and more efficiency from these machines. Inventions included IBM punched cards, and a resident monitor. The punched cards were used as a way of inputting programs and data into the system. The next invention with these cards was to allow automatic job sequencing so that more than one job could be entered into the hardware at once. As for the resident monitor, the idea was to control the hardware so that one job could be entered, started and run to completion, to then transfer control from the job currently being run back to the monitor, and to then allow the monitor to start this process up for another job by commands automatically given by the monitor. This process thereby required a rudimentary operating system to manage the early command and control issues.

Multiprogramming

The next main invention was in the control of memory layout: replacing operating on just one user program to being able to deal with many programs that were loaded in the computer's main memory (at the time, secondary storage had yet to be invented) in order to transfer more efficiently between jobs or programs of the user. This implied a much more complicated operating system, particularly in the area of memory management. The operating systems of the time developed methods for automatically allocating memory positions for pieces of the program and keeping track of these positions. Operating systems are generally thought to begin at this time.

Also, various hardware inventions started to imply additional functions for operating systems. Printers came to see their first use at this time. Although punched cards were still in vogue, other hardware devices, such as disk drives, started to promulgate the computer market, with the requirement that operating systems be able to keep track of program/data, grouped in entities called files on the new disk drives. This led to development of file systems to be able to find the individual files and schemes to keep track of where various files were located on the disks. We will deal with this in more detail later..

Time-Sharing and Parallel Systems

In- the late 1960s and early 1970s, a move away from batch programming to interactive programming took place. This, in part, was driven for more productivity in the use of computers; giving more control to the individual programmer and less to the computer staff was sought. The way in which time-sharing works is that many users at the same time were connected to a mainframe processor. Inventions of CRT displays enabled this move. Individual jobs of the many users were then swapped in and out of memory to have access to the CPU. Once getting access, each job would get a small amount of time; if the job completed, the job would be swapped back to disk and another job would be swapped into the CPU; if the job was not completed, the execution results would be saved and the job swapped out to allow another job to be swapped in. The popularity of this method continued until the early 1980s.

Parallel systems, or multiprocessor systems with more than one CPU in close communication, arose at this time. Strictly speaking, these systems are beyond the scope of this book. However, they were and are important because of the many advantages that they offer: increased throughput, economical, and increased reliability.

Personal Computers

Because of the desire to have communications, control and personal use within a computer, the early 1980s saw the advent of the 'personal computer'. Instead of having a mainframe computer, generally staffed by computer professionals at the central location, hardware was invented so that computers could (and are) be placed on a desk or table so that the non-professional could work with a computer. It took until the early 1990s for these devices to achieve major acceptance; two reasons for this were the invention of e-mail in the late 1980s and the invention of the Web in the early 1990s.

The desktop machine has offered one new paradigm: interaction via graphical user interface, or making use of the pull-down tables, menu bars and graphical icons that populate the display on such machines. Although the functionality isn't new, the method of interaction involves the user in a direct way, which wasn't available across the full functionality of the operating system before this time (even time-share systems had only a few operating system functions available to them). What has happened with the vendor community is that different designs have been coming out very couple of years or so, sometimes with many new functions included (but other times with limited functionality advances). As we are still in (at this writing) in the desktop paradigm, it is difficult to say how and when paradigm shifts will take place.

CHAPTER 3

▼

INTERRUPTS

Communications in a modern processor

Internally in a modern processor, communications is important. This is how information, commands, control features and so on get from one piece of the computer to another. The computer is always started up by going to the low end of main memory and executing the Bootstrap program. This small program loads the operating system into main memory and starts the operating system by going to its first executable instruction and executing. Once we wish to go to the printer, disk, main memory, or other hardware unit, we need a mechanism to access this unit. We also need a mechanism to let the CPU know that a unit has finished its work and control can be changed. Typically, this notification is done through the device controller of the unit (all such devices or units must have a controller). This mechanism is known as an *interrupt*.

Interrupts

The most common function of an interrupt is that the interrupt transfers control to the interrupt service routine (a part of the software in the operating system). This is generally done through the interrupt vector, which contains all the addresses of all the service routines of the operating system. Most interrupt architectures must save the address of the interrupted instruction. In order to prevent conflicts, incoming interrupts are disabled when or while another interrupt is being processed to prevent a lost interrupt. Most application programmers use *traps* in their application programs when they wish to do I/O (either read or write). A trap is a software-generated interrupt caused either by an error or a user request. As such, we say that the operating system is *interrupt-driven*.

It is important that the operating system preserves the *state* of the CPU by storing the contents of the CPU all registers and the program counter in the current routine in main memory; we will discuss this in more detail in the chapter on states.

We should note that some operating systems use different types of interrupts: *polling* and *vectored interrupts*. From a functionality standpoint, both types are the same. However, the direction of control is different: the vectored interrupt sets control by having the operating system itself doing the controlling; polling works by the device setting a flag into its device controller and waiting for the operating system to interrogate the various device controllers to see if there are any messages. Almost all modern systems use the vectored method for efficiency issues.

Two I/O methods exist with interrupts: asynchronous and synchronous. Synchronous works as follows: after I/O starts, control returns to the user program only upon completion (the user program is placed in idle state); asynchronous works in that control returns to the user program **without** waiting for I/O completion. This second method allows a more efficient process and is the method of choice.

A *device-status table* is used for either method of I/O to have information on the state of the various devices when they are being accessed. A figure is located for your use.

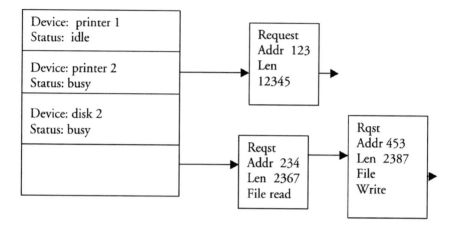

Device-Status Table

One of the important inventions relating to interrupts and I/O is the *Direct Memory Access (DMA) Structure.* This structure is used for high-speed I/O devices that are able to transmit information at close to memory speeds. In this environment, the device controller transfers blocks of data from buffer storage **directly** to main memory **without** CPU intervention. Thus, only one interrupt is generated per block, rather than one interrupt per byte of data/program.

Storage Structure

The computer has a hierarchical arrangement of storage (memory). Closest to the CPU is *main memory.* We note that main memory is the only storage outside of the CPU chip that the CPU can access directly. Next is secondary storage. Secondary provides large non-volatile storage capacity. In all modern machines, *caching* is included, typically between the CPU and main memory on a bus connecting the CPU and main memory.

Consistency is obviously important across the various levels of storage; this consistency may be referred to as *coherency or cache coherency.*

CHAPTER 4

▼

PROTECTION

There are four types of protection inherent in today's machines: 1) dual-mode operation, 2) I/O protection, 3) Memory protection, and 4) CPU protection.

Dual-Mode Operation

Sharing system resources requires an operating system to ensure that an incorrect program cannot cause other programs to execute incorrectly. This, in many modern environments, is implemented by separating system programs from user programs, as a stop gap procedure. This can be accomplished in the following way: at system boot, the hardware starts in a mode called *monitor or privileged mode.* The operating system is then loaded, and starts user processes in user mode. Whenever a trap or interrupt occurs, the hardware switches from user mode to monitor mode (or vice versa). This can be done by the setting or resetting of a bit reserved for this use.

Base and Limit Register

In order for the operating system to protect the hardware and itself from problems arising from multiple interrupts arriving at the interrupt vector almost simultaneously, the vendors today have incorporated two registers onto the CPU chip. The function of these two registers is to determine the legal range of proposed accesses to main memory: they are called:

1. **base register**, which contains the smallest legal physical address in main memory of the program being accessed, and

2. **limit register**, which contains the exact size of the range of the program, typically given in bytes (or words, depending on the architecture of the hardware).

A picture now follows, which illustrated the registers. These registers are calculated in the firmware, when a proposed access is seen by the CPU; at each occurrence, two tests are performed. First, the value of the proposed access is checked against the Base register. If the proposed value is equal to or greater than the base register, we continue to the second test; if not, we trap to the operating system and indicate that an addressing error has occurred. The second test checks the proposed access value against the value of the base register added to the limit register. If the value of the proposed access value is less than the sum of the two registers, we accept that this proposed value is legal; if not, we again trap to the operating system and indicate an addressing error. In addition, when executing in monitor mode, the operating system has unrestricted access to both monitor and user mode; the load instructions for the base and limit registers are privileged instructions (can be run only in monitor mode).

CPU Protection

It is important to protect the CPU from unauthorized use. This is particularly important in academic and similar environments, where occurrence of infinite loops can be a common occurrence in the code of application programmers in the environment. In order to limit useless processing of infinite loops and similar programming mistakes, a *timer* is used to interrupt the operating system after some specified time to ensure that the operating system maintains control. A timer mechanism is implemented through a buffer arrangement in hardware. This is typically the same mechanism that computes the current time on the hardware.

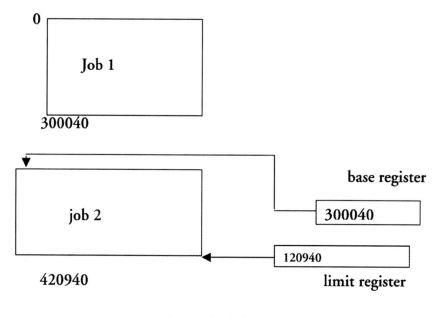

Base and Limit Register

CHAPTER 5

▼

INTRODUCTION TO THE COMPONENTS OF AN OS

Although we will have more to say about the operating system components, it is useful to see the big picture first. We will introduce briefly the main components, and then discuss them in more detail later in the book.

The main components include the following:

1. process management

2. main-memory management

3. file management

4. Secondary storage management

5. Command-Interpreter function.

Process Management deals with *processes.* Such processes include application programs of the users; these processes also include the programs of the operating system itself. From now on, we will use the term, **processes,** to refer to either type of program or software. From our point of view, a process is a program (user-generated or operating system) that is in execution. A process, thereby, needs various resources, including CPU time, main memory, files, and so on to accomplish its task(s). The operating system is made responsible for the functions dealing with these resources such as:

1. process creation and deletion

2. process suspension and resumption

3. mechanisms for synchronization and communication

We will deal with synchronization in its own chapter; whereas the possibility of race conditions exist within any computer; synchronization attempts to eliminate such a possibility and create a stable environment for the operating system. Communication needs certain functionality to intercommunicate between various hardware integral to the single-processor computer, as well as hardware that is attached to the computer to link with other machines (beyond our scope). Dealing with processes (i.e., creation, deletion, suspend, and resume) are dealt with in the next chapter and basically involve the states of a process and how processes rotate from running to not running.

Main-memory management involves the functionality contained within the operating system that

- keeps tract of which parts of the memory are currently being used and by whom
- decides which process to load when memory space becomes available
- allocates and deallocates memory space as needed

File management similarly involves the operating system functionality for:

- file creation and deletion
- directory creation and deletion
- support of primitives manipulating files and directories
- mapping files onto secondary storage.

Secondary storage management involves operating system functionality dealing with:

- free-space management
- storage allocation

- disk scheduling

The Command-Interpreter system was created within the operating system to give availability of commands to the operating system for the above functionality. Such are called command/control statements. This program reads and interprets the various command/control statements so that it can instruct the operating system to get and execute the next command statement. This program is also called the command-line interpreter or shell (in UNIX).

System Calls

Beyond the components of an operating system, system calls provide the interface between the os and the running program. Generally, these calls are sets of assembly–language instructions. Sometimes, specific application languages are designed to provide this capability directly to the user (we have seen one example already–a trap to allow the user to initiate I/O). One other example that is useful to users is the various ways to pass parameters between an operating system and a user program. There are three general ways:

1. pass parameters in *registers*

2. store parameters in a table in main memory, and pass the address of the table as a parameter in a register

3. store (or *push*) the parameters on a *stack* (data structure) by the program and retrieve (or *pop*) the values from the stack by the operating system.

Communication

Internal communication is required on any computer, particularly the passing of messages between various processes, currently active in the computer. There are two ways that this is done: 1) use of shared memory, and 2) direct message passing. In the shared memory case, a portion of main memory is allocated as a single mailbox for one process to drop a message, and another process to access and retrieve the mailbox (and message). As for direct message passing, this is initialed by one process sending a message **via the kernel** and allowing the kernel to address and send the message to the appropriate process. Acknowledgement would go back through the kernel, if needed.

System Generation

Although most of us take it for granted that the operating system is always working for the computer we happen to be working with at the moment, we need to say a bit about the start-up procedure. Operating systems are designed by the vendor to work on a wide variety of classes of hardware and a wide set of implementations (i.e., the hardware that is attached to the specific machine–specific printers, specific number of USB ports, etc.). For this reason, the computer needs to be configured for both each specific hardware site and each specific hardware configuration. This function is generally done at start-up time, each time the machine is powered up. This would then update the machine to any changes that have taken place, since the last power on (this may also explain the function of restarting the computer, after making hardware and software changes). The booting process starts the computer, at the power up, by loading the kernel to the lowest part of main memory and going to the first executable address; the bootstrap program then loads the remainder of the operating system and begins various checks to determine the precise hardware that is configured on the machine currently, will display various graphics on the user output device and otherwise complete the process of getting the processor ready for action.

CHAPTER 6

▼

PROCESSES

As mentioned in the previous chapter, processes are the key to explaining what goes on in an operating system. You recall that both the application programs of a user and the programs of the various parts of the operating system are called processes. A process is a program in execution, and as such, the execution must progress in an orderly fashion, typically in sequential order. We note that, from the viewpoint of the operating system, there may be many processes in "execution" at the same time. But, we also recall, that no two processes can be executing in the CPU simultaneously. This chapter discusses this issue and shows why these two above statements are not in conflict.

Processes

The OS (i.e., operating system) consists of two different types of processes: 1) user, and 2) system. It is clear that a process is an active entity. We note that there may be more than one process for each program. For example, considering the many operating systems using a "windows" metaphor for their graphical display, should we have a number of "windows" representing a number of active programs on the system, this is one example of many processes occupying the system. Or, within Microsoft Word™, we may note that simple typing mistakes are "automatically" taken care of (by having another process checking spelling in the background) or seeing that saving the document occurs every so often (and is denoted by a flash on the display), again showing use of simultaneous processes.

We finally note that a process contains information for its own execution. Typically, it includes the following:

- process state

- program counter
- CPU registers
- CPU scheduling information
- Memory management information
- I/O status information.

This information can be formulated into a **Process Control Block**; it may have the following form:

Pointer	process State
Process number	
Program counter	
Registers	
Memory limits	
List of open files	
. . .	

Process Control Block (PCB)

Process states

Within a process, as it executes, it changes state. The states are as follows:

- **new**: the process is being created
- **running**: instructions are being executed
- **waiting**: process is waiting for an event to occur
- **ready**: process is waiting to be assigned to the running state
- **terminated**: the process has finished execution.

An example of how this might look is given in the following figure.

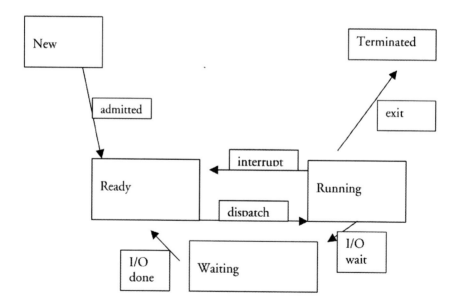

Process State diagram

CPU switch from process to process

The use of these states is in the way in which processes are changed in the way they progress through their execution. If we consider the case of exactly two processes being active, we assume that a process, say process P1, is running and another process, say P2, is ready. P1 will continue to execute until either an interrupt or a system call impacts the CPU. The CPU stops processing P1; the CPU now saves the current state of process P1 and all other needed information into the process control block for P1, called PCB (1). At this moment, the dispatcher (or, dispatch function) within the operating system decides which process, out of those in the *ready queue*, will be next to execute in the CPU (here, there is only one process in the ready queue, P2). P2 is chosen. Once this is known, the operating system reloads (or loads) the information from the current process control block for P2 (PCB (2)). Once the information has been loaded, the operating system goes to the program counter (i.e., the address of the next instruction in this process) and begins execution. We then repeat this procedure at the occurrence of the next interrupt or system call.

In terms of the ready queue, the operating system creates a queue (data structure) which is a list of the processes, in order first-come, first-serve, on the queue. Typically, the queue is implemented with the PCB of the process, so that retrieval of information can be made very fast. In terms of processes that are waiting, they are also implemented by queues established for the I/O device that the process is waiting for. Again, the PCBs of the processes waiting for a specific device are carried by the queue.

Context switch

The term, 'context switch', is used to specify the exact time that it takes to switch from one process to another. This time starts at the instant when we stop processing on the process currently running, and we begin to save the process state and other information into the process control block. The operating system, through the dispatch function, decides on the next process to execute, and the operating system then loads PCB information for the next process to execute. When the OS goes to the program counter, the context switch ends and the time is added up. Clearly, context-switch time is pure overhead; there is no useful work going on during the switch.

Threads

Threads are a type of process. Typically, they are light-weight processes, and may not contain all the information that most processes have in their PCB. The reason for their use is that threads can perform more than one task at a time. One example of this is browsers on various machines. Typically, one thread does the images and another thread does the work processing on the graphical display. Another example is word-processing software where the software does spell-check in the background or the periodic save of text in the background on modern machines. The benefits of threads are their responsiveness, their resource sharing and their economy.

The Dispatcher and scheduling

We have seen from earlier in the chapter that the dispatch function time is the time of the switching context plus the time switching to user mode plus the time it takes to jump to the proper location on the process now being executed. We need to take a closer look at the switching context: particularly the various options available to the dispatcher on how to order the processes in the ready queue.

First-come, first-serve scheduling

Probably the simplest algorithm, the implementation comes directly from the FIFO queue. If we assume that three processes arrive in the order P1, P2, P3, we can compute waiting time. Let us assume P1 requires 24 time units, P2 needs 3 time units, and P3 needs 3 time units; then we see that P1 has 0 wait time (no process delays P1), P2 has 24 units of wait time, and P3 has 27 units of wait time. We can compute the average for comparison with other methods:

Average wait time for FIFO is (0 + 24 + 27)/3 = 17 time units.

Shortest-Job-First (SJF) scheduling

Another way of arranging the processes is shortest job first. If we look at the above assumptions, P1–24 time units of CPU, P2–3 units of CPU and P3–3 units of CPU, we can compute wait time for P1 as 6 time units, for P2 as 3 time units, and for P3 as 0 time units. This would have a average wait time of (6 + 3 + 0)/3 =3 time units. It is a true statement that the SJF algorithm is optimal for a criterion of average wait time

Priority Scheduling

We can associate a priority number with each process. We can then select the highest priority job to run next in the dispatch function. This may not give the best situation for average wait time, but the order of priority will be followed.

CHAPTER 7

▼

SYNCHRONIZATION

The issue that is depended upon more than any other is that execution occurs in an orderly way. This aspect is not as seemingly straightforward as one would like, with operating systems. Part of the problem is that humans think about how application programs work and infer that processes (including both application programs and operating system processes) work the same way. This is not the case, as the following example illustrates.

Let us consider two processes, increment by one and decrement by one. These can be represented in C++ as **++ and --,** respectively. Applying these to a variable, say, **buffer,** we see that implementations of the two processes applied to the single variable, might look as:

Register_1 = **buffer**

Register_1 = *register_1* + 1

Buffer = *register_1,*

Where *register_1* is a local CPU register. In the same way, **buffer**—could be implemented as follows:

Register_2 = **buffer**

Register_2 = *register_2 - 1*

Buffer = *register_2,*

Where register_2 is a local CPU register. Even though we've used two registers, the interrupt mechanism, saving and restoring is done in such a way that we could have done this with only one register.

We now look at how we might interleave these above lower-level statements in some arbitrary order. One such interleaving is as follows, where we assume that the starting value of **buffer** is 5:

Execution 1:   *register_1* = **buffer**   *(register_1 = 5)*

Execution 2:   *register_1* = *register_1* + 1   *(register_1 = 6)*

Execution 3:   *register_2* = **buffer**   *(register_2 = 5)*

Execution 4:   *register_2* = *register_2* - 1   *(register_2 = 4)*

Execution 5:   **buffer** = *register_1*   (**buffer** = 6)

Execution 6:   **buffer** = *register_2*   (**buffer** = 4)

So, we arrive at an inconsistent state; we started with **buffer** = 5, and arrive, after exactly one increment operation and one decrement operation, with **buffer** = 4. We could reshuffle the order of the executions, but we would end up with an inconsistent state e.g., **buffer** could be 6, if we interchange Execution 5 and Execution 6). Such a situation, where the outcome of accessing and manipulating a variable concurrently depends crucially on the order of how the access takes place (and specifically, on the last access), is called a **race condition.** What is done in synchronization (or, more specifically, process synchronization) is to guarantee that race conditions of the kind illustrated above never occur in the operation of an operating system.

Critical Sections

How do we avoid race conditions? The key for this and other conditions is to find a way to prohibit more than one process from reading and writing to the shared data at the same time. This is easier said than done. Or, said another way, we need an *Exclusion or mutual Exclusion*–some way to making sure that when one process uses a shared data file, all other processes attempting to read/write to this file are excluded from doing the read/write.

Formulating this abstractly, we need the concept of a **critical section**–or, a part of a program where shared data can be accessed. In this way, if we can arrange matters such that no two processes were ever in their critical sections at the same time, we could avoid race conditions.

Although this requirement avoids race conditions, this is not sufficient to ensure multiple processes operating at the same time from cooperating correctly in order to share data. We must have the following four conditions holding simultaneously:

1. no two processes may be simultaneously inside their critical sections (mutual exclusion)

2. no assumptions may be made bout speeds or the number of CPUs

3. no process running outside its critical section may block other processes

4. no process should have to wait forever to enter its critical section.

Mutual Exclusion with Busy Waiting

There have been a number of proposals in the literature which claim to achieve eliminating race conditions. We now consider them.

Disabling Interrupts

One proposal is to have each process disable all interrupts just after entering its critical region and re-enable them just before leaving it. Clearly, once interrupts are disabled, no clock interrupts can occur. Since the CPU is only switched from process to process as a result of a clock interrupt, we will never switch from one process to another within this proposal. Thus, we can examine shared data without ever being interrupted by another process.

Suppose we would do this. This could be the end of the system; if we had more than one CPUs, we can only disable the one CPU–the others would or could access the shared data. This is not a feasible solution, and is not implemented. However, it is true that the kernel can disable interrupts for a few instructions when it does some processing. This is not an endorsement for accepting this proposal as a race condition solution.

Lock Variables

Here, we consider a single variable, which is shared, as well as being locked. Initially, the variable is set to zero. When a process wants to enter its critical section, it first tests the lock. If the lock (or, value of the variable) is zero, the process sets the value to one and enters the critical region. If the value of the variable is already one, the process waits and periodically, retests the value. Once the value, upon inspection, is zero, we can have this process enter the critical region.

There is a problem with this proposal. Suppose one process reads the lock (value of the variable) and sees that the value is zero. Before the value can be set to one, another process is scheduled, runs, and sets the variable to one. When the first process runs again, it will also set the value of the shared variable to one, with the result that both processes are in the critical region at the same time.

Strict Alternation

Suppose the variable, *myturn*, initially zero, keeps track of whose turn it is to enter the critical region. Initially, a process 0 inspects *myturn*, finds it to be zero, and enters the critical region. Process 1 now finds the variable to be zero and then begins waiting in its code, continuously testing to see when this value becomes one.

When process 0 leaves the critical section, it sets *myturn* to be one, so allowing process 1 to enter its critical section. So, what we have is an alternating sequence, 010101.... However, Suppose process 1 finishes its critical section quickly, so both processes are in their respective critical sections, with *myturn* set to zero. Now, process 0 executes its loop quickly, coming back to its noncritical section with *myturn* set to one. Now, process 0 finishes its noncritical section and goes back to the top of its loop. Unfortunately, process 0 is not allowed to enter its critical section, since *myturn* is one and process 1 is busy with its noncritical section. So, we run into a problem with this proposal when one of the processes is much slower than the other. The phenomena of sitting in a loop has been given the name of **busy waiting**.

Peterson's solution

There is a solution to the race condition that avoids the traps of the above proposals. First derived by Dekker, then simplified in 1981 by Peterson, this solution combines features of the lock proposal and the alternating turns proposal. The code is now given for Peterson's solution. The code is given in C++.

```
#define FALSE  0
#define TRUE   1
#define  N    2   /* number of processes  */


int turn ;
int  interested [N] ;


Void enter_region (int process)
{  int other;
        other = 1-process;
        interested [process] = TRUE ;
        turn = process;
        while (turn == process && interested[other] == TRUE
}
Void leave_region(int process)
{      Interested[process] = FALSE;
}
```

TSL Instruction

We have other options that rely on the hardware only. One of these is called **TEST-AND-SET-LOCK (TSL).** This operation works as follows. The hardware instruction

Reads the memory word into a register and then stores a nonzero value at that memory address. The operations of reading the word and storing into it must be *atomic*. Atomic here means that this instruction is performed as **one** indivisible primitive hardware instruction, without the possibility of being interrupted, at least until this instruction has completed.

Using this instruction, we consider a shared variable, *flag*, to deal with memory access. When *flag* is zero, any process can set this variable to one and then access the shared memory. When complete, the variable is reset to zero. In order to see that mutual exclusion is attained, start with copying the old value of *flag* to a register and then set *flag* to one. Then, the old value is compared to zero. If it is nonzero, the lock was already set, the program returns to the beginning and retests the lock again. Sooner or later, the value will become zero (i.e., when the process currently in its critical section completes) and the program returns with the lock set. To clear the value in the lock, the program stores a zero in *flag*.

Sleep and Wakeup

Although both Peterson's solution and TSL are solutions for the race condition issue, both have the defect of busy waiting. This both wastes CPU time and can lead to unexpected results. One way to fix this issue is to create interprocess communication primitives that block further processing when the affected processes are not allowed to enter their critical sections. This can be done with the pair **block** and **wakeup. Block** is a system call that causes the caller to block (i.e., be suspended until another process wakes it up). **Wakeup** is the system call that wakes up another process. Both **block** and **wakeup** have one parameter; each have a memory address used to match up corresponding blocks and wakeups.

Semaphores

In 1965, E. W. Dijkstra suggested using an integer variable to count the number of wakeups saved for future use as a solution to the race condition problem. This proposal introduced the new variable type, ***semaphore***. In his original proposal, a semaphore would have the value zero, where no wakeups were saved, or some positive value, where that positive number of wakeups are pending. Given this, Dijkstra invented two operations on the semaphore to generalize the ideas of block and wakeup, namely DOWN and UP. The DOWN operation represents the situation when a process wants to block. The DOWN operation basically decrements the value of the semaphore; correspondingly, the UP operation basically increments the semaphore value, as it generalizes the WAKEUP. These operations have been subsequently been implemented as WAIT and SIGNAL:

```
VOID  WAIT (SEMAPHORE S)

{    value -- ;

if (value < 0)  {

      remove process P from semaphore S ;

block(P);          }     }

void SIGNAL (semaphore S)  {

value ++;

if (value <=   0)  {

      remove process P from semaphore S ;

      wakeup (P);        }      }.
```

These operations, WAIT and SIGNAL, are used to delimit the critical section, when the implementation is in software. Further extending this approach to mutual exclusion, another invention is called **event counters**. Their implementation is similar to the semaphore; their implementation is also similar.

The Producer-Consumer metaphor

Perhaps this is a good place to introduce a metaphor that may help understand the issue of semaphores a bit better. Assume that we have two processes, Producer and Consumer, which have the shared variable, Units_of_Production. The process, Producer, has the operation of producing one unit of production; the process, Consumer, has the operation, consume one unit of production. We see that there are practical issues with this; for example, if we run the Producer process without running the Consumer process, we keep incrementing Units_of_Production to the point of exceeding warehouse capacity; on the other hand, we see that if we run the Consumer process without having any Producer process running, we would keep decrementing the Units_of_Production down to zero (at which point, we can't consume any more; we must build back the inventory in the warehouse by running the Producer process). We see in the case of *Monitors*, our next topic, that this conditional aspect of the processes and where we are on the semaphore can engender a *condition variable*.

Monitors

We have potential solutions to the interprocess communications with semaphores and event counters, but things aren't straightforward. It is possible that processes can be blocked indefinitely, a situation called **deadlock.** Further, it is possible that an error in using semaphores in programs can cause unpredictable and irreproducible behavior. One way around this problem of writing correct programs is another synchronization primitive. One such high-level primitive, invented by Hoare(1974) and Brinch Hansen(1975) is the ***Monitor.*** A monitor is a program construct, in C++ and other high-level languages, which collects procedures, variables, and data structures in a single kind of module or package. Its code is shown below.

Monitors have an important property that makes them useful for achieving mutual exclusion. If we inspect the code, it is clear that only one process can be active in a monitor at any time. Monitors are a special construct within languages; as such, many compilers implement the mutual exclusion code using binary semaphores.

Although monitors provide an easy way to achieve mutual exclusion, that is not enough.

We need at least a way for processes to block when they cannot proceed. The solution comes from the introduction of **condition variables** and the operations (WAIT and SIGNAL) on them. We now return to the Producer-Consumer problem and recall that practical problems arise when the Units_of_Production are zero in the warehouse and we want to consume, or the Units_of_Production equal a full warehouse, but we still want to produce; in both situations, we need to represent these cases in a special way, specifically, by *condition variables.*

For example, when a monitor process discovers that it cannot continue, it does a WAIT on some condition variable, *size.* This action causes the calling process to block. It also allows another process that had been previously prohibited from entering the monitor to enter now. This other process can do a SIGNAL on the condition variable that its partner is waiting on.

An example of a monitor

```
Monitor example
  Integer I ;
  Condition c ;
  Procedure procedure (x) ;

        .

        .


End ;
  Procedure consumer (x) ;

        .

        .

  end ;
  End monitor ;
```

To avoid having two processes active, we have the process doing the SIGNAL exit immediately (this is Brinch Hansen's solution).

Message Passing

For information exchange between machines, we need something else than what has been discussed for mutual exclusion. That something is message passing. This method uses two primitives SEND and RECEIVE, which are system calls rather than language constructs. These calls can be put into library procedures. Some design issues for the message passing include acknowledgement, domains, and authentication.

Equivalence of primitives

One very nice property of all these constructs is that it can be shown that if it can be shown that one construct holds for mutual exclusion, all constructs hold, or are equivalent. In that sense, we have equivalence between: 1) semaphores, 2) monitors, and 3) message passing.

Deadlocks

We have mentioned deadlocks briefly, when in discussing semaphores, we mentioned processes that could not continue; they were deadlocked. Practical examples of deadlocking can be seen from two lanes of traffic, one from the east and one from the west, converging on a single lane bridge or viewing blocks of traffic in Manhattan during Christmas time. In order to talk about the deadlock problem, we now characterize or describe features that characterize deadlocks: the following four conditions must hold simultaneously for a deadlock to occur

a.   mutual exclusion

b.   hold and wait (i.e., process is holding at least one resource and waiting to acquire other resources held by other processes)

c.   no preemption

d.   circular wait.

In dealing with deadlocks, the solution is to find a way that violates one of the above conditions.

Probably the most important piece of the deadlock story is how do we recover from deadlocks. Most of us, particularly those of us using personal computers, tend to abort our systems and restart the computer to avoid deadlocks. If we can, we can try to abort one process at a time until the deadlock cycle is broken. This last method is the preferred one for large data sites, where aborting may result in loss of data that either cannot be replaced or results in unacceptable expense in restoring data. In many cases, we can use various rollback techniques or recovery measures to restore lost data, should we need to abort all or parts of the system.

CHAPTER 8

▼

MAIN MEMORY ISSUES

Main memory is the key to execution of instructions of the machine; the CPU can only work with instructions that are located in main memory. If instructions are not loaded into main memory, this must occur for the instructions to be executed.

Perhaps it is best at this time to review the instruction cycle of all computers. A typical instruction-execution sequence is:

1. program counter supplies the instruction address (i.e., its location in main memory)

2. after the instruction is fetched through a primitive of the operating system or hardware, the register operands are specified as particular fields or portions of a field. For example, the first eight bits are the instruction type and are loaded into the register set aside for the instruction type

3. once the register operands are fetched and loaded into their respective registers, they can be operated on to compute a main memory address that must be accessed for a particular value, or to compute an arithmetic or logic result. Once these calculations have been made, the cycle continues to the next instruction.

Thus, it is clear that, for an application program (of a user or programmer) to be executed, we must load the entire program into main memory, and it must be loaded into the main memory in a way that the instruction cycle can work: in other words, the program must be loaded into main memory in machine-language or assembly language that has a direct interpretation into machine-language. As we see from the previous illustration, the typical processing of a user program converts the high-level language of the program to assembly language code in a load module, but the conversion process also converts (or, maps) the symbolic addresses in the user program into absolute addresses, required by the CPU when executing the instruction cycle. It is this mapping that we will consider in the following.

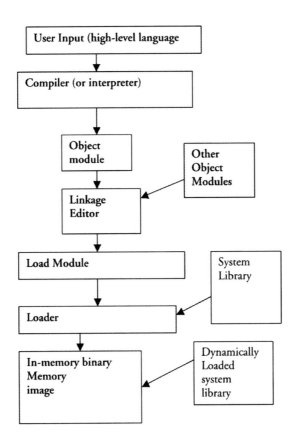

Typical Processing of a user program

Binding of instructions and Data to Main Memory

Binding is really a mapping of one address space into another. For us, we want to map the symbolic addresses (explicit or implied) into actual addresses in main memory that can be accessed by the CPU. There are three steps that are typical:

1. Compile time: If a main memory location is known a priori, the absolute code can be generated; if it is not, the second pass of the compiler resolves all inplied address for the time being, by giving them an explicit designation

2. Load time: If we have unresolved main memory addresses left in the code, we must translate them into *relocatable* addresses (i.e., so many bytes from the start of this module)

3. Execution time: At this point, all remaining relocatable addresses must be translated into main memory addresses. This must be done across all the load modules being combined and all system libraries added to the load module of the original program.

From this multi-step procedure, we are able to create main memory locations from instructions and data of the user program.

We note that there are some hardware aids in this process. One such aid is the *relocation register*. What this register does is add its value (or, the relocation value) to every address generated by a user process at the time the process is sent to main memory. This implies that we can do *dynamic loading*. Dynamic loading means that a routine is not loaded into main memory until it is needed (we can also do dynamic linking in a similar way).

Swapping

A process can be swapped temporarily out of main memory to a *backing store* (or, a pre-specified location on hard disk), and then brought back into main memory for continued execution. The backing store must be a fast disk large enough to accommodate copies of all main memory images of all users and must provide direct access to these images. This main memory management technique has been implemented and modified for many operating systems.

Contiguous allocation

This is the first main memory allocation technique that we have seen. Typically, we have multiple partitions (generally, user programs) to be loaded into main memory. This technique will load the memory positions of the program (containing both instructions and data), starting from the first available main memory position using the relocation register and continuing to load the program into main memory in a contiguous fashion until we are complete. Initially, this will result in main memory being loaded up to a specific main memory position with different partitions. As partitions complete and leave, the previously occupied space for that partition will be effectively empty. This will be called a *hole*. Typically, these holes of various sizes will be scattered through main memory as time goes on. One way to load new processes is to allocate main memory into a hole that is large enough to accommodate the new process. There are a number of strategies that this action can be done:

1. **first-fit:** allocate the first hole (going from the lowest main memory address to the largest) that is big enough

2. **Best-fit:** allocate the smallest hole that is big enough; must search through the entire list of holes to find the smallest hole

3. **worst-fit:** allocate the largest hole; must also search the entire list.

Clearly, in most implementations, Best-fit is the winner.

There are two consequences of the allocation techniques creating holes. **External Fragmentation** is the sum of all holes, considered together. Although it may be possible to use all the space, it is not necessarily contiguous. One way of making this space available is to do a **garbage collection** routine, which will essentially make this non-contiguous space into a contiguous space.

The other implication is that of **Internal Fragmentation.** This phenomenon occurs when the operating system allocates main memory that is slightly larger than requested memory; in this way, holes still exist in main memory and not all space in a partition is used. The reason for this is that many application programs have the capability to dynamically allocate additional memory in their code; provision is made for this, as running the partitions as close together as possible would not allow this code to work.

Paging

The next allocation technique is called *paging*. Within paging, the physical memory is divided into fixed-size blocks, called *frames,* which are contiguous pieces of main memory of size in a power of 2, typically between 512 bytes and 8192 bytes. Then, the logical or user memory is likewise divided into blocks of the same size as the frames in physical memory. These blocks in logical memory are called *pages.* We want to keep track of all free frames. Then, to run a program of size n pages, we need to find n free frames and load the pages of the program into the frames of main memory. To keep track of where things are, we set up a *page table,* which translates the logical address of the pages to the physical address of the frames. This translation typically involves the CPU, the page number of the pages and the page offset. The page number is used as an index into a page table which contains the base address of each page in physical memory. The page offset is a number that is combined with the base address to define physical memory address that is sent to the memory unit. An example is shown in the following figure:

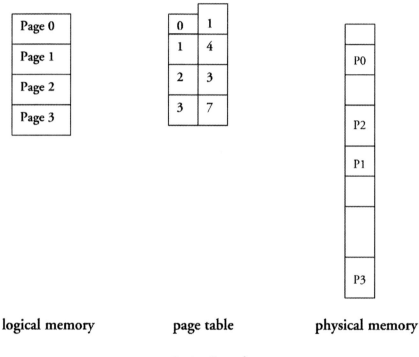

logical memory   **page table**   **physical memory**

Paging Example

So, we see that page 0 converts to frame 1, page 1 converts to frame 4, page 2 converts to frame 3 and page 3 converts to frame 7 from the page table.

We can add another bit to the page table: the *valid(v) or invalid(i) bit*. What this adds to the picture is another entry to the page table is a quick acknowledgement about a page occupying a frame. We would mark the page table with a valid bit where there is a corresponding frame to page, and an invalid bit where there is a free frame (a frame having no correspondence to a page).

Segmentation

This technique is similar to the paging technique just covered. It is said that this scheme supports the user view of memory (or, how the user perceives the pieces of memory from the way in which the program is written). Here, the pages we had in the paging example are replaced by program modules, such as the main program, a procedure, function, subroutine, and so forth. Clearly, in this example, the requirement for equal size is not adhered to. The idea of mapping from segment to frame is similar to the page to frame idea.

CHAPTER 9

▼

VIRTUAL MEMORY

Virtual memory as a strategy has been around since the days when memory was expensive. Although no longer the case, operating systems still incorporate the techniques of virtual memory for the benefits that accrue. When examining real programs, we open up the problems of error conditions, static arrays and files and obscure options and features that can be aided by virtual memory. Additional benefits are that programs are no longer constrained by the size of main or physical memory. More programs can now run concurrently, and there may be less need for I/O with virtual memory.

Virtual Memory continues the paradigm of separating user or logical memory from physical or main memory. If one considers that only part of the program needs to be in main memory for execution at any one time, this opens the possibility of the logical address space of being much larger than the physical address space. This not only allows address space to be shared by several processes, but also allows for more efficient process creation.

We will only consider the situation of *demand paging,* or the case where we only need tyo bring a 'page of a process' into main memory **only** when it is needed. This results in less I/O, a more moderate requirement for memory, and faster response.

The way this works is that when a page (of logical memory) is needed in main memory, there would be a reference to this page from the CPU, as it attempts to access the page in main memory. If this reference fails, the process of accessing the page would abort; this abort would then require the operating system to realize that the page is still in secondary storage somewhere, and would now issue a reference to this page at its secondary storage location and bring it in to main memory. We thus need a valid/invalid bit, which we had in the previous chapter. Here, we need to distinguish between pages in main memory and not in main memory. We will use the definitions: **valid** indicates that the page is legal and in main memory; **invalid** means that either the page is not in logical space or that the page is legal, but not in main memory. What we arrive at is the same page table that we had before. The new item in the process is a **page fault:** if there is ever a reference to a page that is marked invalid, this reference will trap to the operating system, resulting in a call to the operating system to retrieve the page in secondary memory. The steps in handling a page fault would be the following:

A. we obtain a reference to a page from the CPU

B. Checking the page table, we find that an invalid bit is associated with the referenced page. A page fault has occurred. We trap to the operating system.

C. We then retrieve the referenced page from secondary memory through a call by the operating system

D. We bring in the missing page to the main memory, and load it into a empty frame. We then reset the page table to reflect the fact that this page is now in main memory and reset the valid-invalid bit to valid. Finally, we restart the CPU instruction, referencing the page.

Should there be no free frame in this scenario, we would modify our algorithm to replace a page, currently in main memory. This is called *page replacement;* there are a number of algorithms to do the selection of which page is picked for replacement. A further modification is that, to prevent over-allocation of memory by modifying the page-fault service routine to include page replacement. We will add another bit to the page table–a *modify* bit. If a page has been modified while it has been in main memory, we will set the modify bit; thus, if we see the modify bit as set, we will read the page into secondary storage; if not, there is no need to read the page back into secondary storage. The basic page replacement algorithm becomes:

1. After the reference to a page, we locate the page on secondary storage

2. We then find a free frame. If there is a free frame, we use it; if not, we use a page replacement algorithm to select a *victim* frame. After selecting the victim page, we swap this page (if modified) out to its location on secondary storage

3. We now swap in the desired page into the (newly) free frame from its location on secondary storage and then update the page and frame tables to reflect the new page-frame mapping and the new valid-invalid bit

4. We then restart the process, by going to the referenced page.

From the point of view of the machine (and the user waiting for output), we always want to achieve the lowest page-fault rate. The way that algorithms can be evaluated is to execute one on a particular string of main memory references (this is called a *reference string*) and count the number of page faults on that string (assuming that we use a generic string across all algorithms).

Optimal Page Replacement Algorithm

The best that can ever be done is if we knew ahead of time the actual access pattern of pages from now to the future time, we can use this pattern of page references to construct the algorithm for page replacements. The only problem with this algorithm is that we can never achieve it. At the time of the first page fault, the operating system has no way of knowing which page will be executed next. However, knowing this, we can use a hypothetical page reference string to see how good the optimal algorithm can be and measure other algorithms against the performance of the (unrealizable) optimal algorithm.

Not-Recently-Used (NRU) Page Replacement Algorithm

In order to construct an algorithm that is close to optimal, we need to collect useful statistics form the operating system. One way to do this is to use the bits developed for the earlier swapping (i.e., the bit defining whether a page has been referenced (sometimes called the R bit) and the bit defining whether a page has been modified or written to (the M or dirty bit)).

These bits (M and R) can be used to build a simple paging algorithm as follows. When a process is started up, both page bits for all its pages are set to 0 (zero) by the operating system. Periodically (for example, after each clock interrupt), the R bit is cleared, to distinguish pages that have not been referenced recently from those that have been. When a page fault occurs, the operating system inspects all the pages and divides them into four categories, based on the value of their R and M bits:

a. Category A: not referenced, not modified (i.e., R = 0, M = 0)

b. Category B: not referenced, modified (i.e., R = 0, M = 1)

c. Category C: referenced, not modified (i.e., R = 1, M = 0)

d. Category D: referenced, modified (i.e., R = 1, M = 1).

The NRU algorithm removes a page at random from Category A, if A is empty, from Category B; if A and B are empty, from C; and if A, B, and C are empty, from D. The implicit decision

Here is that it is better to remove a modified page that has not been referenced in at least one clock tick than a clean page that is in heavy use. The advantage of using NRU is that it is easy to understand, efficient to implement, and gives a performance that can be reasonably close to optimal.

The First-In, First-out (FIFO) Page Replacement Algorithm

Another low-overhead algorithm is the FIFO strategy. Here, the operating system maintains (typically) a list of pages currently in memory, with the page at the head of the list being the oldest one, and the page at the tail being the most recent arrival. On a page fault, the page at the head is removed (i.e., the victim page) and the new page is added to the tail of the list. We have added an illustration of how this works in practice (below).

FIFO Page replacement

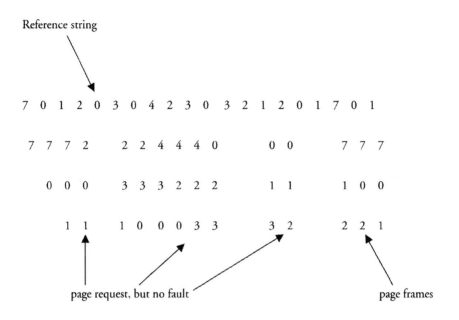

Reference string

| 7 | 0 | 1 | 2 | 0 | 3 | 0 | 4 | 2 | 3 | 0 | 3 | 2 | 1 | 2 | 0 | 1 | 7 | 0 | 1 |

page request, but no fault

page frames

One interesting phenomena is Belady's Anomaly. With a page reference string of 1,2,3,4,1,2,5,1,2,3,4,5, it can be shown that with the number of page frames set at 3, it will take 9 page faults to deal with the above reference string; with 4 page frames, it will take 10 page faults. This seemingly contradicts the logic that fewer page faults result from an increase of page frames (and vice versa); here, with more page frames, we require more page faults. This particular occurrence led to research on why this is so. It has resulted in classes of algorithms sharing the property:

M (m, r) is contained in M (m+1, r), where m varies over the page frames and r is an index into the reference string. This property then says that the set of pages included in the top part of M for a memory with m page frames after r references are also included in M for a memory with m+1 page frames. In other words, if we increase main memory size by one page frame and re-execute the process, at every point during the execution, all the pages that were present in the first run are also present in the second run, along with one additional page.

Least-Recently-Used (LRU) Page Replacement Algorithm

A reasonable approximation to the optimal algorithm is based on the observation that pages that have been used heavily during the last few instructions constitute the set of pages to occur heavily during the next few instructions. From the other perspective, those pages not used in the recent past probably will not be used for a long time into the future. To the extent that this observation is true, it suggests the following algorithm: remove the page that has been unused for the longest time: this is called Least-Recently-Used (LRU).

Although this algorithm is realizable, it isn't very efficient, as it implies keeping a linked list in main memory and manipulating the list on every page reference. One implementation is to keep a counter for every page entry; each time the page is referenced through this entry, we could copy the clock into the counter. Then, when a page needs to be changed, we could scan the counters to determine which pages could be changed. This aging approximation differs from LRU in that aging has a finite number of bits. Suppose two pages each have a counter value of 0; we pick one at random. If a clock tick is about 20 msec., then a page not referenced in 160 msec. probably isn't that vital.

Practical Aspects of frames

It should be apparent that any process needs some **minimum** number of pages to be in main memory to work; if the operating system allocates fewer than the minimum to this process, it can inordinately affect the performance of the process, and thereby, of the entire system. Particularly for the very large memories of today, this wouldn't seem to be an issue; however, in practice, various allocation methods and tuning techniques are used to adjust operating systems to near-to-optimal performance. One notices this when a process doesn't have enough pages. This leads to a page fault rate that is very high, perhaps a page fault every few instructions of the process. This leads to low CPU utilization, as the operating system thinks it needs to change the degree of multi-programming. This occurrence is called **thrashing**. This thrashing is realized when a process is busy swapping pages in and out without performing much useful (if any) work.

What the viability of paging depends on is something called *locality*. Locality is the way in which a running system changes its pages slowly. In other words, the pages in main memory stay static for a while and slowly change into another set of fairly static pages. What this does is suggest that another algorithm, the Working-Set model, can help with this set of slowly-changing pages. Different snapshots of the Working-set, over time, will look very different.

Other considerations go into the selection of pages. It may be that, to enhance performance, we may need to do *prepaging*. Sometimes, the page size selection is affected by fragmentation, table size, I/O overhead and other factors. In some cases, we must lock some pages into main memory; for example, pages that are used for copying a file must be locked from being removed by one of the algorithms discussed earlier.

CHAPTER 10

▼

FILE SYSTEMS

The reason most of us use computers is to locate and retrieve information, usually in a specified format, and then perhaps print or otherwise store this or revised information for future use. We also must be mindful of the fact that main memory of a computer is *volatile*: in other words, it loses its contents between the power down and power up times. We thus need a way of holding or storing the information in a permanent, or *persistent*, way.

All this takes us to the idea of files and ways that we can get to and access files. A file can be termed a named collection of related information that can be recorded on secondary storage. Typically, with today's operating systems, this is the part of the operating system that the users can touch (through the Graphical User Interface, commented on earlier). We now consider the file, its structure, how access can be made and some hardware of interest.

File Attributes

A file is typically named with a string of characters. Along with the name, a number of aspects about this file are collected within its attributes:

- **Name:** the symbolic file name, typically kept in human-readable form

- **Identifier:** a unique tag, usually a number, identifies the file within the file system; typically, this is kept in non-human-readable form.

- **Type:** sometimes called extent of the file

- **Location:** a pointer to a device and to the location of the file on the device

- **Size:** the current size of the file (e.g., bytes, words, blocks)

- **Protection**: information as to who has permission for reading, writing, etc.

- **Time and Date**: Time stamp as to the last time the file was accessed

This information about all files is kept in the **directory** structure that also resides in secondary storage. We will have a few words to say about directories later.

File Operations

The user of computers probably is very familiar with these operations. Typically, a file system includes the following operations:

- **creating a file**
- **reading/writing a file**
- **renaming/repositioning a file**
- **deleting/truncating a file**

Most of the file operations mentioned involve searching the directory for an entry associated with the named file. To minimize the searching, some systems require an *open* system call to be used before the file is first actively used. The operating system keeps a small table containing information about all open files (sometimes called a **open-file table**). When a file operation is requested, the file is specified by an index into this table (eliminating searches). When the file is no longer actively used, it is *closed* by the process and the operating system removes the entry referring top this file from the open-file table.

Additionally, some systems open a file when the first access to this file is made. Most systems require the open command to be made explicit; the search of the directory concludes by copying the directory entry into the open-file table. Then, the *open* system call will typically return a pointer to the entry in the open-file table. This pointer is used in all I/O operations (so, searching is not needed). Typically, a number of items are associated with an open file:

- file pointer
- file open count (counter that tracks the number of opens and closes for each file)
- disk location of the file
- access rights.

Directory Structure

To keep track of files, the file system normally provides **directories**, which, in many systems, are themselves files. Here, we consider directories, their organization, their properties, and their operations.

Hierarchical Directory systems

When a file is opened, the operating system searches its directory until it finds the name of the file to be opened. It then extracts the attributes and disk addresses, either directly from the directory entry or from the data structure pointed to, and puts them in a table in main memory. All subsequent references to the file use this table. Generally, a number of levels of the hierarchy are embedded in the design. In order to group files together in a reasonable way, a general hierarchy is used. In this way, each user can have as many directories as needed.

Path names

When the file system is organized in a general fashion, some way is needed for specifying file names. Two different methods are used: 1) each file is given an *absolute path name*, consisting of the path from the root (or highest level of the directory) to the file, or 2) a *relative path name*, where the file name is taken relative to the current working directory.

Directory Operations

Some of the typical operations are:

- create/delete
- opendir/closedir
- rename
- link/unlink

Implementing files

A number of methods of allocating file storage are available to the operating system. If there is enough space on the secondary storage device, the simplest way to store information is to allocate space as a contiguous block of data on secondary storage. Advantages of this method are: 1) needing only one address for location, and 2) excellent performance. However, there are two disadvantages: 1) need to know the maximum file space a priori, and 2) fragmentation results on the secondary storage device

Another way to allocate space is by **Linked List allocation**. Here, the first physical block of the file will have a pointer; the pointer of the first block will have the address of the second physical block, and so on. Also, **Linked List allocation using an index** an be used to eliminate some of the disadvantages of the Linked List method. Here, we put the pointer word, previously stored in each disk block, and put it into a table or index in memory. Other ways also exist.

Free-space management

Since disk space is limited, we need to reuse the space from deleted files for new files, if possible. To keep track of free disk space, the operating system maintains a **free-space list.** Generally, this list is kept as a linked list, where the head of the list is the first block to be chosen for allocation for a new file; the organization of the remainder of the list are the available pages in order of how the operating system will allocate free pages to requested space.

CHAPTER 11

▼

SCHEDULING METHODS ON SECONDARY STORAGE

This chapter deals with some of the algorithms which schedule access to files that are stored on disk-storage media. In this sense, disk-storage is used somewhat loosely; a disk in our context could refer to a floppy disk, a CD-ROM or a DVD. All these media share the same properties of disk structure.

Disk drives are addressed as large one (1)–dimensional arrays of *logical blocks,* where the logical block is the smallest unit of data transfer between secondary storage and main memory. The 1-dimensional array of logical blocks is mapped into the sectors of the disk media sequentially in the following way:

a. sector 0 is the first sector of the first track on the outermost cylinder

b. mapping proceeds in order through that track, then the rest of the tracks in that cylinder, and then through the rest of the cylinders from outermost to innermost.

The operating system is responsible for using hardware efficiently. Concerning the disk media, this means having a fast access time and disk bandwidth. We see that there are two components of importance when time is concerned: 1) access time, and 2) transfer time. *Transfer time* is the time for the requested blocks to be transferred from the disk media to the buffer in main memory; typically, the user has no control over this variable–the transfer time is constrained by the specific hardware and hardware configuration. However, looking more closely at the access time, we see that this variable has two components itself: 1) *seek time,* or the time for the disk arm (the mechanism that 'reads' the information on the disk media) to move the heads to the cylinder containing the desired sector, and 2) *rotational latency,* or the additional time waiting for the disk to rotate the desired sector to the disk head. Since it is the access time that we can have some control over, we will attempt to minimize the seek time, since the hardware limitation of the selected disk media will have a pre-set value on disk latency. Lastly, we note that the disk bandwidth is the total number of bytes (or words) transferred, divided by the total time between the first request for service and the completion of the last transfer.

Disk Scheduling

We will consider a number of algorithms to schedule the servicing of the disk I./O requests. Let us consider the following example in order to compare the algorithms. Assume the request queue looks like: 98, 183, 37, 122, 14, 124, 65, 67, where there are 200 (numbered from 0 to 199) blocks in the system; we will also assume that the head pointer is currently set at block 53. The first algorithm we consider is First-In-First-Out (FIFO); in this case, we will service the requests in order that they exist in the queue. If we do the arithmetic, we see the total head movement would be 640 cylinders for the example.

The next algorithm to consider is the Shortest-Seek-Time-First (SSTF). The operation of this algorithm is to select the request from the queue with the minimum seek time from the current head position. Here, the total head movement is 236 cylinders.

The third algorithm of consideration is the SCAN (also, the *elevator*) algorithm. The operation of this algorithm is as follows: the disk arm starts at one end of the disk, and moves toward the other end of the disk; the arm services requests of blocks in the queue as the arm passes by the requested sector number. This operation continues until the arm arrives at the other end of the disk, where the head movement is reversed and servicing continues, until the queue is empty. In this case, the total head movement is 208 cylinders.

CHAPTER 12

▼

I/O Systems

The I/O systems residing on a particular hardware configuration are clearly hardware–specific to the hardware vendor(s) involved with this configuration. However, a couple of items tend to be common across vendors to have bearing on operating systems, particularly the design of the software for a particular configuration.

Polling and Interrupts

There is always a communications path between an I/O device and the operating system; the difference is who initiates the communications. In *polling* systems, communication is always started by an operating system command, going to a particular I/O device. The command interrogates the I/O device so determine whether there is I/O waiting at the device that requires attention. If there is no I/O, the operating system will interrogate the next logical I/O device and keep at this interrogation; if there is I/O, the device will send the I/O to be done to the operating system to be serviced; once complete, the operating system will go to the next logical I/O device in its interrogation sequence.

Interrupts work in the opposite way, compared to polling. Interrupts are always generated by the I/O devices and are sent to the operating system to be serviced. The following procedure is typical:

A. the CPU chip has a interrupt request line that indicates to the CPU that an interrupt is waiting

    a. CPU senses the line after each CPU instruction

    b. Once sensing the signal, the operating system then jumps to the interrupt handler routines segment of the operating system

B. the interrupt handler in the operating system receives the interrupts

C. the interrupt vector to dispatch the interrupt to the correct handler routine is generated.

We note that interrupts can be made so that they can be ignored or delayed in some cases.

Application I/O Interface

I/O system calls can encapsulate device behaviors into generic classes. In this way, addition of new printers, for example, can be made generic from the point-of-view of the operating system. We need only the CD for this particular printer to load upon installation, to re-set the operating system to the unique features and/or values contained on the CD. Or, in other words, the device-driver layer hides the differences among I/O controllers from the kernel. I/O devices vary in many of the following ways:

A. character-stream or block

B. sequential or random access

C. sharable or dedicated

D. speed of operation

E. read-write, read-only, write-only

F. blocking and nonblocking I/O

    a. in blocking, the process is suspended until I/O completes

b. for nonblocking, the I/O call returns as much as possible

c. an alternative to nonblocking is aynchronous, where the process runs while the I/O executes

The kernel I/O subsystem includes caching and spooling. Caching is fast memory, typically placed between the CPU chip and main memory. Spooling is the operation which holds output for a device. Typically, spooling is included in operating systems, since a printer can only work on one request at a time.

The operating system can recover from disk read, device unavailable, and transient write failures. A log stores errors as they occur and is used in reporting errors.

CHAPTER 13

▼

THE CLIENT–SERVER IMPACT

It should not be surprising that computer design must grow from the single processor idea when we think to communication and networks. Single-processor ideas stemmed from Von Neumann's "finite-state" machine. This machine was thought of as a piece of magnetic tape, being fed into a tape reader/writer with a control box attached. This control box would permit one character on the tape to be read and analyzed. The control would then instruct the reader/writer to move the tape forward or backward, or would instruct the box to leave the tape in place. In addition, the result of analyzing the tape would produce the next control instruction, for the next movement of the tape as well as what character would be read onto the current entry on the tape or would leave it alone. This model of a computer has remained intact and is the basis for the modern operating systems for single processors. Because of the invention of the printer, keyboard and other I/O devices, most people now look at the computer as a network of various devices doing different functions, requiring communication between the individual devices as well as with the operating system. The design of computers since the 1990s as led to a change of philosophy, enhancing the original Von Neumann thoughts: namely, client-server design.

Client-server (also known as manager-agent), or the client-server paradigm, has seen great growth since the early 1990s. Much of this growth has been supported by the various industry vendors: 1) applications- and data-base providers, 2) operating system vendors, and 3) workstation vendors.

The basic idea of the client-server paradigm is the communications protocol of connecting at least two computers across a network. The protocol defines the kind of communication allowed between the computers at this instant. The "client" computer is the processor which the source of the messaging; the "server" computer is the processor that responds to the "client" in a predetermined way.

The concept

The model of client-server is analogous to many of the ideas in single-processor systems in how such machines do their communication between the various parts of such machines. Thinking about how printer spooling works will illustrate this.

Spooling Operation:

1. An application program performs an "I/O' instruction, by trapping to the operating system

2. The operating system trap collects various parameters of the particular I/O and puts them into an internal stack or data structure. Examples of the parameters are: file name, number of copies, margin details and so on. At times, some of these parameters are added through the display of a page on the user's display and the capture of the input of the user.

3. When the scheduler of the spooler operation allows this stack to continue for printing, the stack is sent to the printer controller for execution. The controller will also translate the characters from how they were stored to the ANSI way in which they will be printed.

4. Control is returned to the operating system, after whatever communication from the spooler operation to the operating system is done. Generally, this involves some message as to whether the operation succeeded or failed.

Two aspects are of particular note: 1) the execution of the printer is completely independent of the end-user, and 2) the explicit mechanism for communication.

These lead to the idea of message passing in client-server systems.

Message Passing

Message passing in client-server systems can be done in a number of ways. However, we will concentrate a process called Remote Procedure Call (RPC). The steps for the RPC are now described.

1. client signals typically through a trap in the application program to the operating system that a message (or processing) is ready

2. transfer of control occurs within the operating system to the kernel of the operating system. Collection of various attributes about the message (or piece of processing) is collected and placed into a data structure within the kernel. Addressing information about the message is now collected by the kernel

3. the kernel sends a message to its domain name server(DNS) to obtain the address of the server that will process the original message of the client.

4. The DNS sends back a reply to the client with the machine address of the server that can do the processing of the message.

5. The kernel appends this address to the message in the data structure and then sends the message to the server

6. Once the server (or destination machine) receives the data structure of the client, the structure is stripped of its information, the information is forwarded to the requested application program by the client, and processing begins.

7. Upon completion of execution, the results are forwarded to the server's kernel for formulation of a return message to the client.

8. Upon receipt of the return message, the kernel of the client forwards the message to the requesting application program.

CHAPTER 14

▼

THE WEB AND ITS RELATION WITH CLIENT-SERVER AND PROTOCOL ARCHITECTURE

The World Wide Web is an invention that has experienced unimaginable growth over the few years since its emergence in the mid-1990s. Its basis is the internet (or Internet), which was invented when networking was in its infancy in the late 1960s. The key with the internet is its incorporation of a protocol that, although not specific among vendors, contains enough commonality that it can be used to transmit and receive (and understand) messages from quite dissimilar computers on a network. This feature has been incorporated into the Web and has been instrumental to its growth.

This chapter continues the story of the previous chapter on client-server and now incorporates the idea of protocol commonality across computers on a network to lead to the invention of the Web in its current form. It should be noted that, at this writing, research and fundamental development is underway world-wide to re-investigate the underlying workings of the Internet (and the Web) and to design more globally robust underpinnings of the Internet and its protocols. This effort is known as Internet 2, and is ongoing at this writing. In so far as this book is concerned, we wish to relate client-server and single-processor operating system concepts to how the Web works.

We start with how the end user perceives the Web, as illustrated in the following figure.

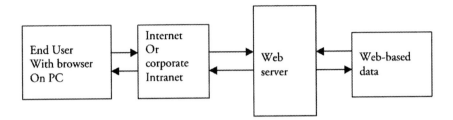

Figure of End-user perception of the Web

What the above illustration shows are the features of the web that are apparent to the end user. The basic idea of the Web is that pages of information are shared, or are "linked', or joined in some way. The end user has access through the web to these pages, via the browser of the end user's machine; this browser is a software program that is running on the end user's computer system. This browser, from the end user's perspective, connects the end user to the Web (or Internet or corporate Intranet) by protocol commands embedded in the browser, and ultimately, achieves a connection to information stored in various sites. The message of this browser requests this information to be transmitted back to itself, by operation of the server on the Web that controls access to such information. This results in the information being sent back to the end user (or client machine), where the browser reformulates this information through its protocol into pages, the typical graphical way in which such information is viewed on the Web. It is noted that Tim Berners-Lee has defined the browser as a web client, and we have used this change of syntax in the above text. We begin to understand the end user perspective as a client-server application where information happens to be in the form of pages (i.e., specially encoded pages). We now consider the overall environment of the

Web in this context, from the point-of-view of the detailed components, enabling the work of the end user.

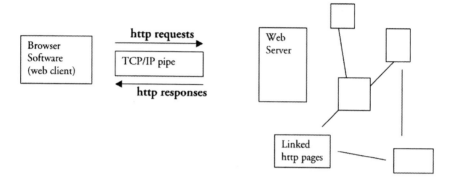

The Web from the point-of-view of its components

Underlying the physical components, there are some basics about the Web. The pages of the web are composed in the hypertext markup (HTML) language. Each page is identified by an address; this address is termed the Uniform resource Locator (URL). This address is unique across all pages linked on all servers across the Internet. As an aside, Tim Berners-Lee, in his book–*Weaving the Web*–talks about the efforts in making the URL, the http and HTML a standard across this network, the Web.

Using the client-server terms to talk about how the components of the Web relate, we see the browser software looks like the operating system functions of RPC (of the client-server paradigm). Such functions form a message, which is to be transmitted to the server. Communication between browser and server occurs in transactions in the form of frames, each having a specific form and content. For the Web (and the Internet), the communications protocol, or the rules of how these frames are constructed, is the TCP/IP protocol

(Transmission Control Protocol/Internet Protocol). Specifically, the routing function of TCP/IP is employed in the transfer of the browser request to the server. The end user is interested in getting "pages", or information, which is displayed through the browser through the HTML language. The http (or hypertext transfer protocol) is used to perform various integrity functions, so that packets of data, routed by TCP/IP, can be integrated into the page structure. In addition, http instructs the browser to display the information in page form on the display device, using the HTML. Put another way, the TCP/IP packets are formed into pages by the http protocol, and the page is translated by the HTML into the "page" on the display, that we have come to know.

The standardization of the language that the pages would be written in HTML, the unique address specifying the location of information comprising what we think of as the pages of the Web, and the protocol glue that routes the packets of information across the network is the infrastructure of the Web. This doesn't imply that something else couldn't be substituted for any or all of the pieces mentioned above. And, it shouldn't be surprising if this occurs in future implementations. But, it is important that any substitutions will occur within the linking of the client-server paradigm and the protocol architecture.

Conclusion

What we have done in this book is derive the basic principles of operating systems and connect these with the issues of client-server and protocol. As we stated in the beginning, this is intended as a beginning; many other texts have looked into more complete descriptions, which was not our intent. It is hoped that the reader may have gleaned enough interest in the various subjects touched on here to continue their investigations.

Bibliography

Operating System Concepts, Silbershatz, Galvin, and Gagne, Wiley, 2003, ISBN 0-471-25060-0.

Modern Operating Systems, Tanenbaum, Prentice-Hall, 1992, ISBN 0-13-588187-0.

The OSI Reference Model, Day and Zimmerman, Proc of the IEEE, vol 71, Dec 1983.

The Working Set Model for Program Behavior, Denning, Comm of the ACM, vol 11, 1968.

Virtual Memory, Denning, Computing Surveys, Vol 2, Sept 1970.

Cooperating Sequential Processes, Dijkstra, <u>Programming Languages</u>, Academic Press, 1965.

Queuing Systems, Kleinrock, Wiley, 1974.

Reflections on software Research, Ritchie, Comm of the ACM, Aug1984.

Computer Networks, Tanenbaum, Prentice-Hall, 1987.

Appendix

Other Books by the author

Network Management into the twenty-first Century, Wiley (formally, IEEE Press), 1994

Introduction to Networks and Telecommunications, iUniverse.com, 2001

Introduction to Business Data Communication with Broadband And Wireless, iUniverse.com, 2002

About the Author

After graduating from Yale, Ohio State, and Rutgers, Phil started a career with Bell Labs, which developed into applied research on protocol design. Phil spent a number of years involved with the TCP/IP and OSI standards, both in domestic and international bodies. Since retiring, Phil Has been teaching at Rutgers, College of William and Mary, and is currently at Hampton University.

0-595-31430-9

CPSIA information can be obtained
at www.ICGtesting.com
Printed in the USA
FSOW02n2158260815
10342FS